Prince of Peace

Bible Verses in this Study are from the following:

Unless otherwise stated all verses are from:

THE HOLY BIBLE, NEW INTERNATIONAL VERSION®, NIV® Copyright © 1973, 1978, 1984, 2011 by Biblica, Inc.® Used by permission. All rights reserved worldwide.

Other Verses are as indicated:

Scripture quotations marked TLB are taken from The Living Bible copyright © 1971. Used by permission of Tyndale House Publishers, Inc. Carol Stream, Illinois 60188. All rights reserved.

Scripture quotations marked HCSB are taken from the Holman Christian Standard Bible®, Copyright © 1999, 2000, 2002, 2003, 2009 by Holman Bible Publishers. Used by permission. All rights reserved.

© 2014 - Veronica A. Litteer - All Rights Reserved

PRINCE OF PEACE

Table of Contents

Opening - Someday My Prince Will Come

Study Instructions

Part I

    1. Peace with God - Fear & Anger
    2. Peace with God - Salvation
    3. Peace with God - Forgiveness

Part II

    4. Peace of Heart - Freedom from Loneliness
    5. Peace of Heart - Relationships with Others
    6. Peace of Heart - Comfort

Part III

    7. Peace of Mind - Freedom from Worry
    8. Peace of Mind - Refuge - Strength
    9. Peace of Mind - Patience - Wait upon the Lord

Part IV

    10. Peace of God - Contentment

Closing

SOMEDAY MY PRINCE WILL COME

I was the youngest of five girls in a family that had just gotten off the welfare rolls in the 1950's. My mother had married my step-father. What a brave man. He married a woman with five girls and one bathroom. Eventually there would be a younger brother.

Since I was born on Easter Sunday, someone in my family wanted to name me Bernadette and then call me "Bunny". I was thankfully named Veronica after St. Veronica whom Catholics believe wiped the face of Jesus on His way to the cross. Veronica means *True Image*. I say, "What you see is what you get."

I have many memories of my childhood....some of them very negative...some quite pleasant.

We lived in the inner city of Buffalo, New York in a predominantly Polish neighborhood. One of the few memories that I have of time spent *alone* with my mother was the day that she took me to see Sleeping Beauty.

I was about nine years old at the time and we had to take a bus to the Buffalo "Downtown" area. The theater was one of those large ornate places with a magnificent chandelier. I was awestruck.

The movie was absolutely enchanting. Seeing it on the big screen was fabulous. Sleeping Beauty, whose name was Aurora, was so beautiful and the Prince was so handsome. And the kiss at the end....Wow!

I also loved the Fairy Godmothers changing Aurora's dress color as she danced with the prince at the end of the movie.

Needless to say this movie made a lasting impression on my little fairytale embracing mind. I wanted so badly to *be* Sleeping Beauty.

Throughout the years, whenever something bad happened in my life, I would say.....Someday My Prince Will Come...and I really believed it. I know that the song "Someday My Prince will Come" is from Snow White. But Snow White doesn't have the emotional effect for me that Sleeping Beauty does.

This Bible Study is about Peace. Peace which is inner contentment; calm; serenity; tranquility. Peace which is harmonious relationships; freedom from hostilities; quarrels, or disagreements.

It was written for the non-believer, the new believer and the seasoned believer. There are 4 parts covering 10 subjects dealing with Peace. These 10 subjects will be intertwined throughout the book. Comfort, Freedom from Worry and Refuge may seem like the same subject. They are similar but still different...as you'll see.   When you're finished, you should have a solid foundation for a life of Peace.

I was 34 years old when I discovered **who** my **Prince** really was and that He **is** my Prince of Peace and He has been with me **all** the days of my life.

Isaiah 9:6

*For to us a child is born, to us a son is given, and the government will be on his shoulders. And he will be called Wonderful Counselor, Mighty God, Everlasting Father, **Prince of Peace**.*

INSTRUCTIONS FOR BIBLE STUDY

Things you'll need or that may be helpful during this Bible Study:

A Bible - I used the New International Version, but formed the questions in a way that you could use most of the Standard versions of the Bible...amplified Bibles can be used but may be confusing.

Writing the verses - I suggest you write the verses because when we write something we remember it better than when we just read it. The written verse can then be used for answering the questions and for later reviewing of the Bible Study. If you can't write the verse, mark the verse in your Bible for later reference.

Writing the verses in your own words - Sometimes this is difficult, but if we can phrase verses in our own words it shows that we really understand the verse. If you find it difficult at first, practice....it gets easier.

A Concordance and/or a **Greek and Hebrew Lexicon**. There are many available for free on the internet.

A Dictionary - a non-religious Dictionary may be helpful.

Read the Definitions at the beginning of each chapter carefully. This will help you to better understand the concept of the Chapter.

Your Feelings - relax - open your mind and heart.

Your Memories - many will be pleasant, some may be painful...all will be helpful.

Personal Application - really try to answer the personal questions. This may help to bring forward areas in your life that you may have trouble with (perhaps refuse to look at) or good times you may have forgotten. In some cases, the answers may resolve hidden issues. In other cases, they may show you that you *have* been truly following the Prince and also that He has been with you all along.

When discussing your personal experiences in a group format, be careful that you don't invade the privacy of others. Be brief. Don't give too many details.

Degree of Difficulty - Since this Bible Study has been written for non-believers, new believers and seasoned believers, there may be questions that seem too easy or too hard. Do the best you can. Group discussions will help clarify the difficult passages. If you're doing this study on your own seek help from a Pastor, other clergyman or seasoned believer.

Prayer - Pray for the Holy Spirit to guide you – before beginning a study session, frequently as you continue and after each study segment.

May God bless you on this journey!

Part I – Chapter 1
Peace with God - Fear and Anger

As a child growing up in the Catholic Church, I thought that God was to be feared. If I or anyone else did something wrong God would be angry and punishing.

The Catholic Church teachings had led me to believe that if one doesn't go to church on Sunday, one goes to hell! When I was young, probably about 7 years old, I was taught that missing church on Sunday was a mortal sin! If you died without going to confession, you would go to hell.

My mother was excommunicated from the Catholic Church because she married again after getting a civil annulment from her first husband. The Church would not give her an annulment unless she paid $3,000-$5,000 along with the request. We were poor and that was an astronomical amount of money in 1957. My mother stopped attending Mass on Sundays, but always insisted that her children attend and behave properly and morally. My mother was a Godly person, as was my step-father.

I loved my mother, and if I was to believe the Catholic Church teachings (which I did at the time), then I had to believe that she would go to hell! It was very hard for me to live with this. I said Rosaries every night and cried myself to sleep for many years. When I was 18, I thought that it just wasn't fair. What kind of God would punish my wonderful loving mother that way? It really wasn't her fault that she didn't go to church. So I turned away from the Catholic Church and . . . . . I turned away from God.

I really didn't understand God. To me, He was quite mean. After fearing my mother's death for so many years, she died when I was 22 and I distanced myself from God even more. Then my brother-in-law died tragically two years later at age 34 and I was really really angry with God.

If God were so heartless that he would take my loved ones, I didn't want anything to do with Him.

Over the years, I often called on God when I was in desperate need but I didn't really think He was listening....let alone would He be willing to help me.

After attending a Christian Church with my husband for several months, I began to learn about a loving God. About His Son, Jesus, who would take away my fear and my anger. One Sunday evening when I was 34 years old, I accepted the Lord as my Savior.

He showed me that He had been with me all of my life. My fear and anger were gone. I knew that my mother was in heaven with our Lord. I didn't need answers to my questions anymore. I just accepted the love of the Lord.

Now the only kind of fear I have for the Lord is the biblical definition of fear . . . reverence, awe, wonder, esteem, deep respect and honor. I'm free from anger because of My Prince of Peace.

BIBLE STUDY

Fear 1 - To be afraid or frightened of; a distressing emotion caused by a feeling of expected danger, evil, pain, disaster, or the like whether the threat is real or imagined; dread; apprehension; anxiety

Fear 2 - Extreme reverence or awe, as toward a Supreme or Higher Power

Anger - A strong feeling of displeasure, hostility, indignation, or exasperation toward someone or something; rage; wrath

GOD'S WORD

I previously thought that God was always watching me so that He could immediately punish me.

Not understanding God's love for me made me afraid of Him. My fear then led me to anger.

God loves us with unfailing love.

1. ✏ Write **Isaiah 54:10**

2. Explain in your own words the meaning of *unfailing love*.

3. What is a *covenant of peace*?

4. What does God feel for us?

There is no fear in love.

5. ✎ Write **1 John 4:18**

6. What drives out fear?

God showed His love for us in an incredible way.

7. ✎ Write **1 John 4:9**

8. How did God show His love for us?

9. What does it mean that *we might live through Him*?

God's love is forever.

10. ✏ Write **Psalm 103:17-18**

11. For how long does the Lord give His love?

12. Who does God Love?

13. What is God's righteousness?

14. What are God's precepts?

God loves those who fear Him.

15. ✏ Write **Psalm 103:11**

16. According to the second definition of the word *fear* listed at the beginning of this chapter, explain this verse.

Anger is for fools.

17. ✏ Write **Ecclesiastes 7:9**

18. What is the definition of the word *fool*?

19. ✏ Write this verse in your own words

There are limits to anger.

20. Read **Ephesians 4:26**

21. ✏ Write this verse in your own words.

The Lord tells us about anger.

22. Read **Psalm 103:8-10** and then read it again.

PERSONAL APPLICATION

23. Are you or have you ever been *afraid* of God? When and Why?

24. Have you ever been *angry* with God? When and Why?

25. What makes you angry?

26. If you do get angry, how do you handle your anger?

27. Are there times when anger is justified? If so, give an example.

DIGGING DEEPER

28. Are there other verses that can help one to overcome the negative *fear* of God?

29. Are there other verses that can help one to overcome anger?

SUM IT UP!

30. In a few words, what does this chapter say to you about Fear & Anger?

Part I - Chapter 2
Peace with God - Salvation

In Chapter One, I mentioned that I let go of my anger and accepted the Lord as my Savior. There was a lot more than anger that I had to release. Over the years, I had built a wall around my heart to protect it. I was afraid of being hurt again. The loneliness of my childhood, the fear of losing my mother, betrayals by friends, broken romances and many other heartaches led to a very strong wall.

In my mind and heart, I didn't need anyone. Not even God....least of all God. But God had other plans for me. He brought Buck into my life. Buck had come to know the Lord through his own emotional hardships. Shortly before we were married, he had given his life to the Lord. I wasn't aware of this event but I did notice a change in him. Rather than being in emotional turmoil, he seemed to *be at peace.*

He asked me to marry him which was a great surprise to me because before his surrender to God, he told me that he didn't even want to think about marriage for at least 10 years. That was OK with me because I wasn't very interested in marriage. I was too independent and there was that *wall.*

But, I loved Buck very very much and so I said yes. At the time I was working for a funeral home and Buck and I had met a Baptist minister who said something that touched Buck's heart during a funeral service for one of my co-workers. We asked that minister if he would marry us.

During the pre-nuptial interview, Buck told the minister that he wanted God to be part of his marriage.

I told the minister that I did _not_ want the word "obey" in the vows and I also did _not_ want "till death do us part" in the vows. I'm sure you can read between the lines of that request. We were married, had a wonderful honeymoon and started our life together.

After we were married, Buck would read his Bible and listen to Christian radio. He would come home and tell me what he had read or heard. He piqued my interest. In other words, the Holy Spirit was starting to work on me via my husband. We started to attend the church that was founded by Rev. James Andrews, the Pastor who had married us.

We attended services on Sunday mornings and evenings and on Wednesday evenings. At the end of each service, the Pastor would give an "altar call". He would pray the sinner's prayer and invite those who wished to give their lives to Christ to come down to the front and pray with him. One question he would ask was, "If you died today, went to heaven and Jesus asked you why He should let you in, what would you say?" I had a variety of answers for that question, but none of them seemed quite good enough to get me past the pearly gates.

In order to answer the "altar call", I thought that I had to hear angels sing or some kind of music with lights flashing. I also thought that it had to be planned ahead of time. So I was surprised one Sunday evening to find myself walking down the aisle without having given any thought to what I was doing. As I reached the Pastor, he held my hand and asked me what he could do for me. All I could squeak out was, "I want to break down the wall." Pastor Andrews handed me over to an Associate Pastor who would pray with me. I have no idea what the man said.

I just sat in darkness with a light shining in front of me. When the light faded and the darkness left, the congregation was gone and the church was empty except for Buck and the Associate Pastor.

It was like I was floating on a cloud for weeks after that. Revelations came pouring into my mind and heart. The Holy Spirit was alive and working in me.

I felt like an enormous weight had been lifted. The wall was no longer there. I wasn't angry at God. I didn't need to know why my mother and brother-in-law died. I had *peace*.

By surrendering my heart and soul to the Prince of Peace, making Him the Lord of my life, I was not only at Peace with God; I was at Peace with Myself.

BIBLE STUDY

Salvation - Deliverance from the penalty and power of sin and its spiritual consequences, membership in the body of Christ and admission to eternal life in the Kingdom of Christ.

John 3:16 *- "For God so loved the world that He gave His one and only Son, that whoever believes in Him shall not perish but have eternal life.*

GOD'S WORD

God wants everyone to be saved.

1. ✏ Write ***John 6:40***

2. Who is God's Son?

The following verses are commonly called the Roman Road to Salvation. They may be familiar to you, but let's "really" look at them.

All have sinned.

3. ✏ Write ***Romans 3:23***

4. What is sin?

5. What does it mean to *fall short of the glory of God*?

6. ✏ Write this verse in your own words.

Salvation is a gift.

7. ✏ Write **Romans 6:23**

8. What is a gift?

9. What does the phrase *wages of sin* mean?

10. ✏ Write this verse in your own words.

God demonstrated His love for us.

11. ✏ Write **Romans 5:8**

12. Define the word *love*.

13. ✎ Write this verse in your own words.

We must believe and confess.

14. ✎ Write **Romans 10:9-10**

15. What does it mean to *confess with your mouth?*

16. Define the word *Lord*.

17. What does it mean to be *saved?*

18. ✎ Write this verse in your own words.

We are saved by grace through faith; it is a "gift" of God.

19. ✎ Write **Ephesians 2:8**

20. Define the word *grace*.

21. Define the word *faith*.

Jesus Christ died so that we would have peace.

22. ✎ Write **Isaiah 53:5**

PERSONAL APPLICATION

23. Have past experiences in your life caused you to build a wall around your heart?
    What were they?

24. What did you do or what can you do to break the wall down?

25. Do you know anyone who has a wall? What can you do to help that person?

26. If you died today, went to heaven and Jesus asked you why He should let you in, what would you say?

27. If you are saved, describe your salvation experience.

28. If you have not given your life to Christ, what are you waiting for? No wall is so big that God cannot shatter it. Stop now. Open your heart. Pray for the Lord to guide you. Speak to your Pastor about your desire to seek the Lord.

DIGGING DEEPER

29. Find other verses in the Bible regarding Salvation?

SUM IT UP!

30. In a few words, what does this chapter say to you about Salvation?

Part I - Chapter 3
Peace with God - Forgiveness

Forgiveness is a vital element in our ability to have Peace with God. Forgiveness played an important part in my life in many ways but especially in one major event that hindered my relationship with the Lord for over 10 years...it was the loss of my mother.

My mother was, I believe, a Godly woman who made some bad decisions in her life. I believe that she felt much guilt for those decisions, couldn't forgive herself and she didn't think God would forgive her either. She became an alcoholic. I think the drinking helped her to forget. She died of cirrhosis of the liver at age 51. Her death was one of the reasons that I became so angry at God.

When my mother was diagnosed with cirrhosis of the liver, the doctors thought that she would not last more than about 3 months. But, almost a year later, my mother was hospitalized. My step-father received a call from the hospital in the middle of the night when my mother had taken a turn for the worse. The family gathered at the hospital and we were allowed to spend 15 minutes with her...two people at a time.

During that 8 hour vigil, there was a statue of Jesus in the waiting room and I remember staring at it all night long. I didn't realize until years later just how much comfort I was given by the presence of that statue...the image of my Prince of Peace who was with me during that time of trial.

When my mother died that morning, I couldn't feel anything. I couldn't even cry. I was numb. The chores of arranging the funeral, contacting relatives, etc. were distributed among my sisters and me.

The next few days were filled with family visitations, reminiscing about the wonderful qualities of my mother and the good times we had with her and what she meant to us all.

I remember thinking about God and based on my Catholic Church beliefs, I wondered if she was in heaven. After all, I was told that she wouldn't be. Would God forgive her for not attending Mass on Sundays? I certainly couldn't forgive God for letting her die.

My sisters saw my mother just before she closed her eyes for the last time. One told me that my mother said, "Jesus is coming for me." Another sister told me years later that my mother had looked up into the corner of the room near the ceiling...there was a smile of contentment on her face and she said, "He's so beautiful." We believe it was Jesus that she saw. We believe that God forgave her and took her to live with him in Paradise.

I've done things in my life for which I felt that God could never, ever forgive me. Even after becoming a Christian, I still felt unworthy in God's eyes. It took me years to realize that none of us is worthy. There is no sin too great for God to forgive if we are repentant and but ask.

Luke 23:34
Jesus said, "Father, forgive them,
for they do not know what they are doing."

While dying on the cross, my Prince of Peace asked God to forgive those who crucified Him; how can I *not* forgive others and myself.

BIBLE STUDY

Forgive - To stop feeling anger or resentment toward someone; To stop blaming; To absolve from payment of a debt or obligation; To pardon

GOD'S WORD

God's Word tells us that our loving Father forgives us all our sins but one.

1. ✎ Write **Matthew 12:31**

2. What sin does God not forgive?

3. What does blasphemy against the Spirit mean?

God forgives our sins.

4. ✎ Write **Isaiah 43:25**

5. Explain the words *for my own sake.*

God removes our sins.

6. ✏ Write **Psalms 103:12-14**

7. ✏ Write these verses in your own words.

We are born with a sinful nature. But when we accept Christ as our Lord and Savior, we become new creations.

8. ✏ Write **2 Cor 5:17**

9. What must we do to become a new creation?

    This verse tells us that as Christians, we become a new person. We change. We're not the same. That doesn't mean that we don't sin. But with the help of the Holy Spirit, who convicts us of our sin, we're less likely to sin...and if we do we're usually repentant.

****

    Remember my "wall". My wall was in the form of a *stone heart*. The following verse confirms that the Lord replaced that *stone heart* with a *heart of flesh*. The Holy Spirit continues to work in me to help me stay in God's Will.

God gives us a new heart.

10. ✏ Write **Ezekiel 36:26-27**

11. What does God give us in addition to a new heart?

12. What does God take away from us?

13. What does God want us to do?

14. ✏ Write this verse in your own words.

***God forgives us
but He expects us to also forgive others.***

That is not a suggestion, it's a command.

God's command regarding forgiveness.

15. ✏ Write **Matthew 6:14-15**

16. What will happen if you don't forgive others?

PERSONAL APPLICATION

17. Is there something that you need to ask God to forgive you for?

18. Is there something that you need to forgive yourself for?

19. Is there something that you need to ask someone else to forgive you for?

20. Is there something that you need to forgive someone else for?

DIGGING DEEPER

21. Can you think of someone in the Bible who really needed and received Forgiveness? Tell about it.

22. Are there other verses that tell us that God forgives us?

SUM IT UP!

23. In a few words, what does this chapter say to you about Forgiveness?

Part II - Chapter 4
Peace of Heart - Loneliness

As a little girl growing up in the Catholic Church, I went to Mass each weekday and on Sunday. In those days, the Mass was said in Latin and to me it was mostly boring. So I would read the Parables.

My favorite parable was the one about the Shepherd looking for His lost sheep. There was a picture of Jesus holding a lamb. I always imagined that I was that lamb. As the youngest of the five girls, I was sometimes excluded from going places and doing things that my sisters did. Other times, they were forced to *drag* me along with them. I was known by some of my sisters as the *spoiled brat*.

As the youngest, I was given more attention. I was also very cute and I think I deserved it. ☺ But seriously, I was painfully shy and frequently lonely. My mother and step-father worked evenings and I often had to go to sleep alone in the house while my sisters were outside in the yard or watching television.
It was one of those "afraid of the dark things" that I still have not fully overcome.

The thought of Jesus holding me in His arms like the sheep was so very comforting. It still is.

Because of being the youngest in my family, I often asserted my leadership outside the house. With my friends, if I couldn't be the leader, I didn't want to play. I was often the leader, but there were times when someone would rebel and I was left home alone....once again on the outside.

Even though now I can see that it was my own fault that I had no one to play with, as a child I just felt abandoned.

As I grew older, I often felt that I was not a part of what was going on around me. Mine was the era of hippies, psychedelics, free-love, pot smoking, etc. I never bought into that whole scene, but I did have friends who were part of it. They didn't harass me and they did allow me to be with them, but I was the odd one...still alone.

I have had several close friends who eventually proved to not be such "good" friends. I treat others as I would like to be treated. That treatment was not always reciprocated and I was often taken advantage of. Betrayals by friends had also helped to build *my wall*.

When my husband and I got married, we used the phrase "Today I Will Marry My Friend" on our invitations, cake, napkins, etc. After many years of wedded bliss, we are not only husband and wife, we are the best of friends.

Through the years whenever I felt lonely, I would remember the "Lost Sheep" and there was something, at the time unidentifiable, that said to me, "It's OK. I'm here with you".....and I would feel *at peace*.

No matter how far I wander away or how lost I get, my Shepherd, my Prince of Peace will always find me and welcome me home to be a part of His family. I am "never" alone.

BIBLE STUDY

Alone - Apart from other people; single; solitary; having no one else present; separate or isolated from others; excluded from all others; by oneself

Lonely - sad, dejected, depressed, disheartened or dispirited by the *awareness* of being alone or apart from other people

GOD'S WORD

The Lord is our Shepherd.

1. ✏ Write **Matthew 18:12**

2. What does this verse tell you about our Lord....*our Shepherd?*

We have a friend in Jesus.

3. ✏ Write **John 15:15**

4. What does Jesus call us?

5. What is the definition of the word *friend?*

Jesus is with us.

6. ✎ Write **Matthew 28:20b**

7. When is Jesus with us?

8. How long will He stay with us?

God is with us.

9. ✎ Write **Hebrews 13:5b**

10. How long will God be with us?

11. Define the world *forsake*.

"I will never leave you nor forsake you!"

This quotation is one of the most emphatic statements in the New Testament. In Greek, it contains two or more double negatives, similar to saying in English....

"I will never, no never, no not ever leave you nor forsake you."

PERSONAL APPLICATION

12. Can you recall an experience as a child when you felt alone?

13. Can you recall an experience as an adult when you felt alone?

14. John 15:15 as stated above says that Jesus calls us *friend*. How does this make you feel?

15. Have you ever had or do you now have a *very good friend?*
    What is your best memory of that friend?

16. I have heard it said that in order to *have* a friend, you must *be* a friend.
    What kind of things can you do to *be* a friend?

17. Do you feel God's presence with you?

18. What can you do to feel God's presence?

DIGGING DEEPER

19. Are there other verses in the Bible that you use to overcome loneliness?

SUM IT UP!

20. In a few words, what does this chapter say to you about Loneliness?

Part II - Chapter 5
Peace of Heart -
Relationships with Others

The Christmas Season has always been very special to me. Most of my fondest childhood memories are of Christmas with my family. We always had a family gathering. Since there were five girls and one boy plus husbands, boyfriends, children and often other family members and visitors, the total participants would range from 12 to 30 people.

Christmas Eve was our special day. There were several years when we celebrated by having different nationality Christmases every year...which included Polish (our heritage), Italian, Mexican, French, and Irish to name a few. We would eat the foods of that country, wear their colors, and even perform some of their traditions. For the Christmas of 1976, we all agreed to "hand-make" our gifts to each other and wear red, white and blue.

One of our favorite traditions was the singing of the "12 Days of Christmas". We each had our standard verse which we would sing individually or in pairs and then all join in on "and a Partridge in a Pear Tree". My brother-in-law and his daughter always sang "Five Golden Rings" and never failed to make us all laugh with their not so slightly off key rendition.

As the family extended to nieces and nephews and their families, it became more difficult to celebrate on Christmas Eve, but we all made an effort to have the family gathering on a day close to Christmas. The tradition still stands.

Because I live in another state now and my family is in the Buffalo area, I haven't been able to be there in person, but I try to call them on the day they are gathering and I am with them in spirit....and they send me pictures.

Since Christmas has always meant so much to me, it is fitting that the Bible verse that announces the coming of Jesus Christ should be the verse that introduces Him as my Prince of Peace.

Isaiah 9:6
For a child will be born to us, a son will be given to us; And the government will rest on His shoulders; And His name will be called Wonderful, Counselor, Mighty God, Eternal Father, **Prince of Peace***.*

There was a period of time (about two years) when I was not welcome at traditional family gatherings. My family is mostly Catholic and I was attending a non-denominational Bible believing church which I think made some members of my family uncomfortable. They did not understand.

Early on in my Christian walk, the Holy Spirit impressed some verses upon my heart that gave me comfort and encouragement. They still do to this day.

Mark 10:29-30
"I tell you the truth," Jesus replied, "no one who has left home or brothers or sisters or mother or father or children or fields for me and the gospel will fail to receive a hundred times as much in this present age and in the age to come, eternal life."

Luke 14:26
"If anyone comes to Me and does not hate his father and mother, his wife and children, his brothers and sisters—yes, even his own life—he cannot be my disciple."

Clearly, the Lord had prepared me for a time of separation from my family...and He also gave me *peace* in my heart. I knew when the separation came that it was only temporary and that soon I would be welcomed into the family again.

One of my sisters eventually called me and apologized for her behavior which had caused the family to exclude me. We cried and expressed our love for each other and have remained closer than ever.

Jesus does not want us to *hate* our loved ones. In this context, *hate* expresses *priority*. Jesus wants us to put Him first in all things.

As the Prince of Peace, Jesus is the ruler of His domain. The word *peace* has many meanings. All of which we strive to attain. I've come to learn that Jesus is the only one who can give true *peace*.

BIBLE STUDY

Relationship - An emotional connection between people; the way two or more people behave toward each other

Peace - A state of harmony between people or groups; reconciliation

GOD'S WORD

Peace be with you.

1. ✏ Write ***John 14:27***

2. Who gives us *Peace*?

3. What does Jesus tell us to "not" be?

Others will hate us.

4. ✏ Write ***Mark 13:13***

5. What does this verse tell us?

Love one another.

6. ✏ Write **John 13:34**

7. What does God command us to do?

8. How are we to love others?

9. How does God love us?

Love your enemies.

10. ✏ Write **Matthew 5:44**

11. What does God tell us to do about our enemies?

More about loving your enemies.

12. ✏ Write **Luke 6:27-28**

13. What else does God tell us to do about our enemies?

Do onto others.

14. ✏ Write **Luke 6:31**

15. How are we to treat others?

More instructions about our enemies.

16. ✏ Write **Luke 6:35**

17. How are we to treat our enemies?

18. What is our reward?

19. How does God treat the ungrateful and wicked?

20. What does this tell you about God?

PERSONAL APPLICATION

21. Was there a time when your beliefs separated you from others?

22. Was there a time when someone didn't understand something you said or did?

23. Think of someone with whom you don't have a good relationship. What can you do to improve that relationship?

24. What can you do to show love to others?

25. God showed His love by sending His Son to die for us. What does "Christmas" mean to you?

26. Can you remember a very special Christmas?

27. Do you have any family traditions?

28. Do you have a Christmas tradition that shows love for others? If not, can you think of a Christmas tradition that you could do in the future?

DIGGING DEEPER

29. What other verses tell us about what our relationships with others should be?

SUM IT UP!

30. In a few words, what does this chapter say to you about Relationships?

Part II - Chapter 6
Peace of Heart - Comfort

My step-daughter Lynne was expecting her second child. She was 4 months pregnant when she started to have problems. One day the doctor said she was doing fine. The sonogram showed us a tiny baby girl. The following day, Lynne started to have pains. The doctor checked her again and put her on bed rest. But the next day, Lynne was rushed to the hospital.

Macy Jordan went home
to be with the Lord on May 3, 2006.

A virus had attacked Lynne's amniotic fluid...and Macy died in-utero. God provided us with an incredibly compassionate nurse. The nurse, knowing the heartbreak that Lynne was feeling, brought Macy to her wrapped in a little blanket with a rose on top of it. Lynne was able to hold Macy. It was not easy for her. Her dad and I were so proud that she could handle such heartache. As I held little Macy in the palm of my hand, my heart was also breaking. I felt the loss of never being able to watch this precious little one grow to womanhood. But, this palm-sized little angel will not be forgotten...because the Lord says:

Isaiah 49:15-16 - I will never forget you. See, upon the <u>Palms of My Hands</u> I have written your name.

I know that Macy is with the Lord and safe in the Palm of His Hand.

The day of Macy's memorial service was bright and sunshiny...not a gray cloud in the sky. Just as the loved ones gathered on the rear deck of the family home above us there appeared a small white cloud and from it spread a beautiful "rainbow".

We all felt that it was a sign from God.

Lynne, whose faith in God remained strong even through her heartache, asked her father, "Why would God trust me with something like this?" God never gives us more than we can handle. He promises to be with us and to be our strength and our comfort.

God not only writes our names on His palms, He also *holds us* in the hollow of His hands. In our pain, He gives us comfort. God even sent a sign to us...*a Rainbow.* He also sent a special blessing....

Jordan Marisa

I believe that God gives us all a sign that He is with us and all will be well. I also believe that there is a blessing in even the worst of tragedies. It may not seem so at the time, but . . . . . .

Close to the day that Macy would have been born, Lynne became pregnant and God blessed His creation with a beautiful healthy baby girl the following May. Jordan does not replace Macy because Macy still lives. Jordan is another of God's blessings.

Our beloved Owen has not forgotten his little sister. Two years later on May 19, 2008, Owen who was 4 yrs. old, told me, "My sister Macy died and went to heaven and she's with Jesus. Macy is Jordan's big sister and my little sister. I have two little sisters."

We all will never forget Macy Jordan. My Prince of Peace provided us with two Princesses, a heavenly one and an earthly one.

BIBLE STUDY

Comfort - to soothe in time of grief or fear;
to console;
a state of ease or well-being

Comforter - one who comforts

GOD'S WORD

God knows us.

1. ✎ Write ***Jeremiah 1:5***

2. How long has God known us?

Blessed are those....

3. ✎ Write ***Matthew 5:4***

> God gives his Children a *special* comfort
> in their times of sorrow or grief.

Rejoice in the morning.

4. ✎ Write ***Psalm 30:5***

5. What does *His favor* mean?

6. How long does it last?

7. What does *weeping may remain for a night but rejoicing comes in the morning* mean?

God of all comfort....

8. ✏ Write **2 Corinthians 1:3-4**

9. What is God *the Father* of?

10. What does this verse tell us to do?

Come unto Me... find rest for your soul.

11. Read **Matthew 11:28-29**

12. ✏ Write these verses in your own words.

PERSONAL APPLICATION

13. Have you ever felt that God set you apart from others? In what way?

14. Describe a time of grief in your life.
    How did you feel about God at that time?
    Did you feel God's comfort?

15. Did you or can you find the sign from God in that time of grief?

16. What blessing did God eventually give you?

17. What are some of the burdens in your life that God can help you with?

18. Other than in times of grief, describe a time in your life that you felt God's comfort.

DIGGING DEEPER

19. Do you have other verses that you use when you need God's comfort?

SUM IT UP!

20. In a few words, what does this chapter say to you about Comfort?

Part II - Chapter 7
Peace of Mind - Freedom from Worry

My mother was a wonderful woman. She was a strict mother who didn't let her children get away with anything. You know...the mother with the eyes behind her head. When we were young we never left the house without kissing her and she would say in Polish..."Go with God" and we would say in Polish "Stay with God." As we grew older, it was just the kiss and my mother had changed the traditional saying to "I trust you and God is watching."

Wow, was that powerful. My mother was no dummy. She knew what she was saying. I loved her and desperately wanted her to always trust me. And, the Catholic Church had taught me that God was always watching. I thought He was a mean God waiting to punish me at the drop of a hat.

For the most part, I was a very good little Catholic girl...though I did have my moments. I may have told a little white lie here or there which caused great anxiety for me until I could go to confession. If I died before then, I would surely go to hell.

Are we not all worriers? Just look at all the synonyms for the word "Worry".

Worry - To be anxious, feel uneasy, be apprehensive, be disturbed, be troubled, be distressed, agonize, fret, despair, lose heart, be downhearted, be heavyhearted, be afraid, dread, brood over, stew, be concerned, misgiving, consternation, dismay, trouble, bother, grief, anguish, torment, agony, misery, woe, difficulty, care, vexation.

Wow! How many of those feelings do we experience every single day of our lives? Lots!

Before I gave my life to my Prince, when I worried it would often overwhelm me.

For example, when I was in my early 20's, I had an apartment and a job. One day circumstances caused me to quit my job and soon after I was told that I was being evicted from my apartment for selling Avon products. I was in despair...worried about what I would do...where I would live, etc. I told my sister about my situation and that night I threw myself on my bed and said, "God, help me. I don't know what to do." Remember, this was when I was still angry with God. But in my despair, I called on Him anyway.

The next morning, my sister called me after telling my step-father about my situation. He told her that he wanted me to come home to live with him and my younger brother. I would not have asked him if I could come home, I was too embarrassed.

There were other times in my life, when I had called on God and He was there. And times that I didn't call on God and He was there. Looking back on my life as I said in the opening of this book, my Prince of Peace was always with me when I needed Him. After all, it's what He promises all His children.

Now let's talk about the real issue here! How do we get Freedom from Worry...Peace of Mind?

TRUST! TRUST IN GOD!
No matter what our circumstances are, we're to "trust" the Lord. We're to place ourselves in the hands of the Prince of Peace and have confidence that all will be well because He is *always watching us.*

BIBLE STUDY

Trust - To have faith in, To believe, To rely on, To depend upon, To count upon, To place oneself in the hands of, To assume, To expect, To hope, To be confident, To be certain.

To Trust means to have "confidence in". To believe in the powers, trustworthiness, or reliability of a person or thing.

Worry - to feel uneasy or anxious; torment oneself with or suffer from disturbing thoughts

Synonyms for worry - be apprehensive, be disturbed, be troubled, be distressed, agonize, despair, lose heart, be downhearted, be afraid, be heavyhearted, dread, brood over, stew.

GOD'S WORD

We must have a steadfast mind.

1. Read the following 3 versions of **Isaiah 26:3**

New International Version
You will keep in perfect peace him whose mind is steadfast, because he trusts in You.

The Living Bible
He will keep in perfect peace all those who trust in Him, whose thoughts turn often to the Lord!

The Holman Christian Standard Bible
You will keep in perfect peace the mind that is dependent on You, for it is trusting in You.

2. What does God promise us?

3. To whom does God promise *perfect peace*?

God is always with us.

4. ✏ Write **Exodus 33:14**

5. What does God's *presence* mean?

6. What does God promise to give us?

Call on God.

7. ✏ Write **Psalm 86:7**

8. When should we call on God?

9. What will He do?

Jesus tells us not to worry.

10. Read **Matthew 6:25-34**

11. What are we to worry about?

12. Why are we not to worry?

Trust in the Lord.

13. ✎ Write **Proverbs 3:5-6**

14. What does this verse mean?

Do not be anxious about anything.

15. ✎ Write **Philippians 4:6-7**

16. What does God tell us to do when we're anxious?

17. In your own words, what is the result?

PERSONAL APPLICATION

18. What do *you* worry about?

19. Was there a time in your life when you turned a problem or worry over to God?
    What was the result?

20. Was there a time in your life when a trust was betrayed? Has this been resolved? If not, what can you do to resolve it?

21. Do you have anything now that you need to *trust* God with?

22. Who in this world besides God do you trust?

23. What must you do in order to be free from worry?

DIGGING DEEPER

24. Are there other verses that help to keep you from worry?

SUM IT UP!

25. In a few words, what does this chapter say to you about Worry?

Part III – Chapter 8
Peace of Mind - Refuge & Strength

In Chapter 6, we studied Peace of Heart – Comfort. In Chapter 7, we studied Peace of Mind – Freedom from Worry. It may seem that "refuge" would fall into those categories. But to me refuge is something much more intense then comfort or peace of mind. It also involves conquering fears and being strong.

I mentioned previously that when I was young I was often lonely, shy and full of fear. Not only was I afraid that my mother would die, I was afraid of everything...people, the dark, failure, illness, death, loneliness, making decisions.

When I was a little girl, my sisters would call me a cry-baby so I began to hide my fears. I couldn't let them know how I felt. This also contributed to *the wall*.

To this day, I still sometimes feel that I have to be tough. I can't cry. I can't show weakness. I can be compassionate, but not weak. There is still a little part of *the wall left*. I'm working on that.

I remember a time when I was about 8 years old. I walked to school every day and on the way to school I had to pass a house that had a small dog that would run out and snap at my feet as I walked. I was terrified of this dog. I would run and he would chase me. Then I started to walk all the way around the block so that I wouldn't have to pass that house.

I told my older sister about this and she said she would walk me to school. She told me that if I didn't show fear, the dog wouldn't bother me. So as we passed the house with the dog, I didn't show fear and the dog didn't snap at me.

I didn't show fear because my sister was by my side. After I became a Christian, I learned that I had nothing to fear with Jesus by my side.

Now, I trust the Lord. But sometimes, in my human nature, I try to be strong on my own....silly girl.

When I began to study the Bible, I found so many wonderful promises that God has made to us. He promises to protect us...to be our refuge...our strength.

My favorite refuge verses:

Deuteronomy 31:6
"Be strong and courageous. Do not be afraid or terrified because of them, for the LORD your God goes with you; he will never leave you nor forsake you."

Psalms 91:4
"He will cover you with his feathers, and under his wings you will find refuge; His faithfulness will be your shield and rampart."

What a comforting image that is! I don't have to be strong. God is strong for me. He will never, no never, no not ever leave me or forsake me. I can just nestle under His wings. I can even cry if I want to....which I often do since becoming a Christian..... especially when I hear a glorious hymn like Amazing Grace. I carry lots of tissues in my purse now when I go to church.

I have exchanged my *wall* for a R*ock and a Fortress*. In my Prince of Peace, I trust.

BIBLE STUDY

In Chapter 1, we defined the word fear as reverence, awe, wonder, esteem, deep respect and honor. We also defined it as fear of someone. In this chapter, we will study fear in general.

Fear - To be afraid or frightened of; a distressing emotion caused by a feeling of expected danger, evil, pain, disaster, or the like whether the threat is real or imagined; dread; apprehension; anxiety

Strength - the quality or state of being strong; physical power; intellectual or moral force; power by reason, authority, or resources; power of resistance.

Refuge - shelter or protection from danger or trouble; a place of safety; a place to go for aid, relief, or escape.

GOD'S WORD

Overcoming Fear – Being Strong – Seeking Refuge

God goes with us.

1. ✐ Write **Deuteronomy 31:6**

2. What does God tell us to be?

3. What does God tell us not to be?

4. What is the definition of the word *forsake?*

5. When will God forsake us?

The Lord is my Rock.

6. ✏ Write **Psalm 18:2**

7. Write your thoughts about each of the following as they relate to you and God.
   Do as many as you can.

   a. Rock

   b. Fortress

   c. Deliverer

   d. Shield

   e. Horn of Salvation

   f. Stronghold

The Lord is my refuge.

8. ✏ Write **Psalm 91:2**

9. Who are we to trust?

10. ✏ Write this verse in your own words.

We are to love the Lord.

11. ✏ Write **Psalm 91:14**

12. Why does the Lord rescue and protect us?

13. What does it mean to acknowledge the Lord's name?

The Lord cares for us.

14. ✏ Write **Nahum 1:7**

15. Who does the Lord care for?

Psalm 46:1 – God is our refuge and strength, an ever-present help in trouble.

16. What does the phrase *ever present help in trouble* mean to you?

PERSONAL APPLICATION

17. Do you think it's OK to cry? Why or why not?

18. When was the last time you cried?

19. What do you think fear does to us?

20. What must we do to overcome fear?

21. What, in life, do you fear?

22. Do you remember a time when you felt that you had to be strong on your own?

23. Do you still feel that you have to be strong on you own? Yes _____ No_____

    If your answer is no...Where do you get your strength?
    If your answer is yes...Why? What can you do about it?

24. Look at the definition of *refuge* at the beginning of this Study Chapter. Have you ever sought *refuge* in the Lord? Write about it.

25. Can you recall a time when the Lord helped you overcome a fear?

DIGGING DEEPER

26. Can you find other verses that show God as our strength or refuge?

SUM IT UP!

27. In a few words, what does this Chapter say to you about Fear, Strength and Refuge?

Part III - Chapter 9
Peace of Mind -
Patience & Wait Upon the Lord

There are verses in the Bible that I call my *life's* verses....my *everyday* verses. They are called to my mind by the Holy Spirit as needed...which seems to be quite often.

Psalms 46:10 - Be still, and know that I am God...

This verse has to do with my personality. I tend to want to control things...maybe everything. I can be a bit of an over-achiever. Remember, I am a new person since accepting Christ as my Lord and Savior. No longer too timid and fearful, I often step out of my comfort zone while holding on to the hand of My Prince. God gave me the gifts of teaching and administration. Maybe it's not my fault that I want to run everything. ☺

Though I can be a follower, my natural tendency is to lead. This brings me to the topic of this chapter. PATIENCE - Wait Upon the Lord

I tend to run with an idea or thought. I don't always take the time to consult with my Lord. I think I have to be ready to handle anything that could in any way (even remotely) happen. I have to have plan A, B and C....sometimes even Plan D.

I was attending a ladies bible study and happened to run across the need to explore my favorite verse, Psalms 46:10, mentioned above. In doing so, I had a wonderful *goose-bumpy* revelation. When I translated the words, *Be Still*, one of the definitions for the Hebrew word H7503 - râphâh (raw-faw') contained the word *Relax*.

The verse to me now says:

*Relax and admit to yourself that **God** is in charge of your life!*

I really don't have to be in charge of everything every minute of the day. It's not easy for me to relax, but I'm working on it.

Another verse that helps and also goes along well with the first is...

Isaiah 40:31 *- but those who hope in (wait upon) the LORD will renew their strength. They will soar on wings like eagles; they will run and not grow weary, they will walk and not be faint.*

There are times when I may get tired and weary just thinking about some of the things that I have to do during the course of a day, a week, etc.

I sometimes want to just hide under the bed. But if I remember to *wait* for the Lord to lead me...He gives me strength, takes away my weariness and helps me to walk steadily.

I can just be patient, relax and know that everything will be right because my Prince of Peace is in control.

BIBLE STUDY

Patient - Capable of bearing delay and waiting for the right moment.

Patience - The capacity of calm endurance.

Wait - To remain inactive or stay in one spot until something anticipated occurs.
To remain or be in readiness or expectation
To depend upon.

GOD'S WORD

Be Still....

1. ✎ Write **Psalm 46:10**

2. If you can, look up the Hebrew word that is translated *be still*.

3. ✎ Write this verse in your own words.

Wait Upon the Lord.

4. ✎ Write **Isaiah 40:31**

5. If you can, look up the Hebrew word that is translated *hope in* or *wait upon*.

6. ✎ Write this verse in your own words.

Wait patiently.

7. ✎ Write **Psalm 37:7**

8. What does this verse mean to you?

9. Read **Psalm 27:14** - Fill in the blanks

Psalms 27:14 -_ _ _ _ for the Lord; be strong and take heart and _ _ _ _ for the Lord.

10. Read **Psalm 40:1** - Fill in the blank

Psalms 40:1 - I waited _____ for the LORD; He turned to me and heard my cry.

NOTE: WE ARE TO *WAIT PATIENTLY* FOR THE LORD

PERSONAL APPLICATION

11. Applying the definitions at the beginning of this chapter with the previous verses, do any of the verses take on a new meaning for you? Do they reinforce your previous understanding of the verses?

12. Do you have trouble with patience...waiting for the Lord's timing?

13. If yes, give an example.

14. Do you take the time to *Be Still* and listen to the Lord? How do you do this? If you don't do this, how can you start to do this?

15. Was there a time when you *didn't* wait for the Lord to guide you? Tell about it.

16. Was there a time when you *did* wait for the Lord to guide you? Tell about it.

17. What are some of **your** favorite *life's verses* and/or your *everyday verses*? Why?

DIGGING DEEPER

18. Can you find other verses or Biblical examples that speak of patience?

SUM IT UP!

20. In a few words, what does this chapter say to you about Patience and Waiting Upon the Lord?

Part IV - Chapter 10
Peace of God - Contentment

We've covered many types of Peace in this book and now for our final chapter, we explore the Peace *of* God.

The Peace *of* God is so supreme that we as humans will never completely understand it but we can experience some of it. It will guard and protect us spiritually. But, as the verses below will tell us, we must have faith, righteousness, obedience and thankfulness.

Faith - Believing that Jesus Christ is the Son of God who died for us and was raised from the dead, and accepting Him as our Lord and Savior assures us of an eternal place in heaven. Our salvation is secure and not based on works.

Righteousness - There is more that is expected of us as Children of God. We are to be righteous...which means our conduct should be blameless. We must behave in all ways that are pleasing to God.

Obedience - We are also to follow His commands and bear fruit. To *abide* in Christ is to live with and for Him continually and to remain steadfast and faithful to Him...to accept without question or opposition all that Jesus commands.

Thankfulness - We are to acknowledge that all good things come from God. All we have is a result of God's benevolence.

How do we know what is expected of us? What are God's commands? What is pleasing to God?

The answers to these questions are in the Holy Scriptures. God explains it clearly to us in His Word. We must *stay* in His Word...study it diligently with the help of the Holy Spirit.

One of my gifts from God is the ability to organize. I'm known by many as the "Spreadsheet Queen". When I first started to study the Bible, I thought it would be a great idea to write a detailed outline of each Chapter. I thought it would be very helpful to others. Don't forget I was raised Catholic, never studied the Bible and never went into a Christian book store. Wow, was I embarrassed when I discovered all the scholarly books written over the centuries by the greatest minds in Christendom. And there I was thinking I had an original idea. What a pea-brain!

I have so much to be thankful for. I thank Him continuously throughout each and every day.

I acknowledge that everything I am and everything I have comes from the Lord; even the parking spot near the door at the supermarket or mall. Nothing is ever too small to be grateful for. But, I'm still having trouble being grateful for spiders.

To sum it up, if we abide in Christ, the result will be the Peace of God. The confidence in knowing that while on earth, we have a place of refuge, a sense of completeness, quietness, tranquility, contentment and a special *friendship* with God the Father and the assurance that we will dwell with Him and spend eternity with our "Prince of Peace".

BIBLE STUDY

Contentment - not desiring more than what one has.

Peace of God - the tranquil state of a soul assured of its salvation through Christ, and so fears nothing from God and is content with its earthly lot.

GOD'S WORD

Faith and Righteousness.

1. ✐ Write **Romans 5:1**

2. Read **Romans 3:21-24**

3. Review your definition of faith from Chapter 2.

4. What is the definition of the word *righteousness*?

5. Where does righteousness come from?

6. Who are we to have faith in?

The Fruit of Righteousness....

7. ✎ Write **Isaiah 32:17**

8. ✎ Write this verse in your own words.

Remain in Christ.

9. ✎ Write **John 15:4-5**

10. What do the words *remain in* or *abide with* mean?

11. ✎ Write this verse in your own words.

Obedience.

12. ✏ Write **Luke 11:28**

13. What is the definition of the word "obey"?

14. ✏ Write this verse in your own words.

*OBEDIENCE IS THE EARTHLY OUTWARD
PROOF OF OUR FAITH.*

Be Thankful.

15. ✏ Write **Colossians 3:15**

16. What is the definition of the word Thankful?

The Peace of God.

17. ✏ Write **Philippians 4:7**

18. Write this verse in your own words.

PERSONAL APPLICATION

19. In what other ways besides our Salvation can we demonstrate faith?

20. Name some things we can do to please God.

21. List other things for which you are thankful to God.

DIGGING DEEPER

22. Are there other verses that promise you Contentment and the Peace of God?

SUM IT UP!

23. In a few words, what does this chapter say to you about the Peace of God?

CLOSING

John 10:27-28
My sheep listen to my voice;
I know them, and they follow me.
I give them eternal life, and they shall never perish;
no one can snatch them out of my hand.

I use these verses often. I try to be patient and follow the Lord's commands....His voice. And...I feel comforted that I am being held in the hand of my Prince of Peace and that no "one" or no "thing" can take me away from Him. Verse 28 is like my security blanket. I don't think I ever had a "blankie" as a child.

Years ago, I read that "no one can hurt me without my consent." Perhaps in light of John 10:28...
no one can hurt me without God's consent.

Throughout this book, I used the words "My" Prince of Peace.

Jesus is "Our" Prince of Peace...Mine and Yours.

2 Thess 3:16
Now May the Lord of Peace Himself
Give You Peace
At All Times and In Every Way.
The Lord Be With All of You.

Made in the USA
Middletown, DE
04 February 2022